DOES MY CAT HATE ME?

DOES MY CAT HATE ME?

Improve Behavior, Boost Health, & Mend Your Bond With

Environmental Enrichment

By

Amy Shojai, CABC

A Quick Tips Guide, Vol. 5

FURRY MUSE

Furry Muse Publications
Sherman TX 75091-1904

© 2019 Amy Shojai

ISBN-13: 978-1-948366-18-2

PUBLISHER'S NOTE
Every effort has been made to ensure that the information contained in this book is complete and accurate. However, neither the publisher nor the author is engaged in rendering professional advice or services to the individual reader. Further, veterinary medicine and animal behavior science continually evolve. The ideas, procedures, and suggestions contained in this book are not intended as a substitute for consulting with your pet's physician. All matters regarding your pet's health require medical supervision. Neither the author nor the publisher shall be liable or responsible for any loss or damage allegedly arising from any information or suggestion in this book.

The scanning, uploading and distribution of this book via the Internet or via any other means without the permission of the publisher is illegal and punishable by law. Please purchase only authorized electronic editions, and do not participate in or encourage electronic piracy of copyrighted materials. Your support of the author's rights is appreciated.

Publisher: Furry Muse Publishing
PO Box 1904
Sherman TX 75091-1904

TABLE OF CONTENTS

DEAR CAT LOVER 9
CAT ENRICHMENT, WHAT DOES IT MEAN? 10
   TERRITORY 12
   FOOD 16
   CARE 17
   PURR-SONALITY 24
ENVIRONMENTAL ENRICHMENT 29
   VERTICAL SPACE 32
   HORIZONTAL SPACE 35
      LITTER BOX LOCATION 36
      SUN WORSHIPERS... 37
      FURNITURE LURKERS..................................... 39
   HITTING THE MARK 40
COMPANIONSHIP 44
   AFFECTION ON KITTY'S TERMS 44
   KNOW KITTY'S PREFERENCES......................... 45
   CAT-TO-CAT (AND OTHER) COMPANIONS..... 47
   TIMESHARE MENTALITY...................................... 48
   SAFETY ALWAYS!.. 49
FEEDING ENRICHMENT 50

HEALTHY "EXTRAS" FOR FELINE FUN 54

FEAR FREE TRAINING 58

    VISITING MONSTERS 59

    CRATE EXPECTATIONS 60

    CLICKER TRAINING FOR CONFIDENCE 61

THANK YOU FOR READING! 64

ABOUT AMY SHOJAI 66

DEAR CAT LOVER,

After writing 30+ pet behavior, vet care and training books, preserving "the bond" remains paws-down the most important goal of my career.

Preserving the pet-owner bond is why I wrote my quick-tips guide series. The cat behavior advice is easy to do and will help your "pet love" grow as your family grows.

You can find lots more free cat-centric advice by subscribing to my Bling, Bitches & Blood Blog at AmyShojai.com. You can also subscribe to the free Pet Peeves newsletter and my ASK AMY YouTube. Stay tuned for some upcoming feline-tastic care and behavior webinars! Find my books here.

I love hearing what kind of furry info-tainment readers love best—yes, I do answer email! Please write me at amy@shojai.com. Or find me on Twitter (@amyshojai) as well as on Facebook. And now—read on for paw-some cat-egorical indoor enrichment tips for your cat's health and happiness.

Purrs,

Amy Shojai

CAT ENRICHMENT,

WHAT DOES IT MEAN?

For those of us who love our cats—and who doesn't?—ensuring they stay healthy and happy is job one. But how do we do that? Certainly, a veterinarian figures prominently in the equation.

But the vet doesn't live with your cat. You are responsible for day-to-day feline care, and today we know this goes beyond plopping food in a bowl or scooping the litter box. One of the hottest trends in cat care today references "environmental enrichment." But just what does that mean?

Is it play with specialized toys? Is it attention, or high-dollar cat trees, or motorized feeding gadgets? Yes and no—and it depends on your cat. I know that's vague, but it really does come down to the individual feline's needs.

Environmental enrichment addresses not just WHAT the cat wants, but HOW to provide for these needs. Just as high-dollar food does no good if the cat snubs the bowl, environmental enrichment only works when these changes satisfy and engage the cat's desires. To understand how presentation impacts cat health, it's important to look at things from the cat's perspective.

WHAT DO CATS WANT?

Before we get into the nuts and bolts of cat-centric enrichment, it's important to put ourselves in the cat's viewpoint. What does the cat want? What does the cat need? Sometimes it can help to quite literally get down on all fours and examine your home from the cat's-eye-level.

Once we figure out what the cat wants and needs, we can delve deeper. Environmental enrichment positively impacts our cats' emotional and physical health, and the cat's relationship with us.

Feline wants and needs overlap. They can be defined in just a few broad categories.

1. territory
2. companionship
3. food
4. care & shelter
5. safety (freedom from fear)

How we provide for each of these depends on the individual cat. Still, some generalities apply to most cat companions.

TERRITORIAL ISSUES

- "I own this!"
- Familiarity
- Safety
- Protection

A cat's territory goes beyond claiming ownership of a given area or object. As both predators, and prey themselves, cats rely on familiarity of their environment to provide them with safe and comfortable places to live. Claiming territory allows Kitty the ability to predict what to expect and prevent the unexpected.

Cats have both a home range where they live, and a much larger territory that they patrol and defend. A male cat's territory may be up to 10 times larger than a female cat's range and territory. This is especially true for intact kitties. How far the cat travels depend entirely upon the resources available, so an area with abundant food may reduce the size of the cat's home range and territory. Outdoor cats may cover several miles each day.

The home range must be free of danger, so a cat can hunt, eat, rest, and mate without fearing attack. A safe environment must offer a place to sleep, access to food, safety to rear offspring, and a way to defend these resources from interlopers. A kitty might want a tree within her territory as a safe lookout or perch beyond the reach of strange dogs, for example. Ideal cat territory offers access to water, a warm dry place to hide kittens, a sunny spot to nap, and maybe a private area to toilet and mark ownership without interruption. In some instances, feral cats agree to share their home range with a few relatives, and together they defend these resources against danger.

Many companion cats in the United States live exclusively inside. That protects them from the physical dangers of strange animals, car accidents, parasites and disease. But when we restrict the natural home range and territory of the cat to a mere handful of rooms, we inadvertently promote problems. Households with multiple cats may notice this even more. Such cats act out with hit-or-miss litter box tactics, express anxious or aggressive behaviors, or exhibit health challenges exacerbated by stress.

When the resources must be shared between multiple cats, or the cat feels unduly restricted in this artificial home range, environmental enrichment becomes even more important. Compared to the outdoor "natural" cat lifestyle, cats want and

need MORE territory than we can provide. The question then becomes, "How can we make their environment less stressful?"

COMPANIONSHIP

- Humans
- Other Pets

In addition to territory, companionship also impacts what the cat wants and needs. Cats certainly express affection and love toward family members, including humans. But we can't know if cats love us the same way we love them. They certainly don't express affection like humans.

Cats are designed to be solitary hunters. It's hard, after all, to share a communal meal of one single mouse. But cats are not necessary solitary by choice. Even feral kitties develop and maintain close relationships with other cats, particularly with related female cats. They display acceptance and affection with mutual grooming and body rubbing to share scent, or peaceably resting near each other.

Companion cats can bond very closely with each other. You may see these relationships at shelters, with bonded pairs that may pine away if not adopted together.

Again, the companionship and relationship aren't restricted to other cats or people. My own Karma-Kat deeply mourned the loss of his canine friend. After Magical-Dawg died, Karma slept with the dog's collar for two weeks, constantly rubbing his face against the leather that still held his friend's scent.

Oftentimes, we're not aware of the depth of a kitty relationship. Cats show their affection and interactions more subtly, sometimes in ways difficult for humans to perceive. Sharing the same room, or resting on opposite ends of the same couch, may be your cats' equivalent of a declaration of adoration.

It's important to understand how cats express love and affection and to reciprocate, but on the cat's terms. Cats are not primates, like us, and may not appreciate touchy-feely hugs. They still enjoy our companionship and accept our love and affection when we understand their terms.

FOOD

- "I'm hungry!"
- Hunting & Foraging Fun
- Filling the Bowl
- Garfield Glutton vs. Finicky Feline

Food brings on the purrs in cats. Whether you have a Garfield glutton or a finicky feline, nutrition means life-or-death for cats. Feeding cats goes beyond filling the bowl, though. Offering food *appropriately* can provide an incredible emotional benefit to cats that goes beyond satisfying tummy hunger.

Cats, by nature, are predators. We've sequestered them inside our homes, controlled what and how they eat, and many have become couch potatoes. Some cats only exercise by strolling from the sofa to the bowl, and back again. What a missed opportunity! Mealtime can enhance their relationship with you, with each other, and with their environment. In other words, create a more natural way to feed cats, as part of environmental enrichment.

Many cats already find supplemental feeding on their own. My little old lady cat, Seren-Kitty, loved hunting crickets; she always left the drumsticks behind for some reason. Many cats enjoy or even prefer hunting for their food. That doesn't mean you must offer mouse entrees, though.

Today, we can use foraging techniques based on the new (actually old-fashioned!) way of feeding cats. That helps cats become healthier both physically and emotionally. For kitties that have put on too much "table muscle" and tend toward obesity, enriching the environment using meal feeding techniques accomplishes multiple positive results.

CARE

- "I need HELP!"
- Grooming
- Exercise & Play
- Prophylactic
- First Aid
- Geriatric Assistance

Modern cats live longer, healthier lives than ever before. The care options available make all the difference. It's up to us, as their advocates, to ensure they get proper veterinary help.
But it goes beyond annual vaccinations and preventative care.

When cats roamed the great outdoors, they attended to their own grooming. Today, of course, some of those longhaired beauties need human help to stay spiffy. Neither can we neglect playtime for cats, as it's great exercise and a part of the care they need.

Providing first aid in case of emergency (once Seren snagged a claw, ouch!) means we humans must know what to do at home. Even more important, we partner with caring veterinarians to maintain kitty health, and offer geriatric assistance as they get older.
Too often, cat owners skip veterinary visits when the cats become fearful and stressed. Part of the care we should provide includes teaching cats how to accept important medical help. Reducing stress and fear, and choosing great veterinary

partners, has become vital. Enriching the cat's home environment can make a positive difference with this, as well.

SAFETY (FREEDOM FROM FEAR)

- "Stranger Danger!"
- Recognizing Triggers
- Preparation & Training
- Reducing Angst

Fear and uncertainty increase cat stress. Being scared increases the potential for physical health issues, too.

There's a reason for the term "scaredy-cat." I call it stranger-danger and write about this in nearly all of the Quick Tips booklets. This instinctual response offers self-protection for cats.

Suspicion of anything unfamiliar keeps cats alive, rather than approaching something potentially dangerous. For that reason, cats prefer to hide or stay a safe distance away from anything that's strange or new to them.

If they're inside a small room, they can't run away. No control over the environment increases stress. Cats that can't run from danger become defensive and may either shut down emotionally or become aggressive to make the scary person or thing go away.

When perception of THREAT > perception of CONTROL, resulting STRESS causes physical & mental health to suffer.

It comes down to ***threat*** versus ***control.*** Dr. Tony Buffington, a brilliant researcher on feline health and behavior, explains the concept in this way. When the *perception* of threat is greater than the *perception* of control, your cat feels stress. That stress can elevate both physical and mental concerns that in turn impact the cat's health.

Focus here on the word *perception*. Is the danger real? It doesn't have to be real. If the cat believes danger threatens and the cat has lost control of the situation, the stress escalates. Increased stress can result in all kinds of health and emotional issues from missing the litter box to digestive upsets. Stressed cats may eat too quickly in a race with other felines, and then vomit the food right back up.

When we take our cats to the veterinary clinic, we thrust the cat into a strange environment. There are scary sounds, smells, and strangers touching and poking them. All these things elevate the cat's fear—and a fearful cat can't think logically, even if she wanted to. Increased stress can affect blood and urine test results, which also makes the doctor's job more difficult to diagnose and treat appropriately.

"Stressed cats react with sickness behaviors— they hide, vomit, refuse food, and snub the litter box."

Dr. Tony Buffington,
The Indoor Pet Initiative.

Heart Disease	Dental Disease
Kidney Disease	Thyroid Disease
Obesity	Diabetes
Gastrointestinal Disease	

In order to lower kitty stress levels, we must find ways to build and encourage cat *confidence*. To do that, learn to recognize triggers that cause fear in cats. You likely already know many of them—the sound of the garbage truck, or the neighbor dog barking, or one cat bullying another. With preparation and behavior training we can relieve or even eliminate some of these triggers. Environmental enrichment is vital today more than ever for our cats, especially those confined exclusively indoors.

NEUROTICISM

SHY: More hiding spots & quiet spaces

BOLD: Cautions for bold/adventure-cats

PURR-SONALITY MATTERS

There's not a one-size-fits-all plan for a cat's environmental enrichment. As we know, not every cat is the same. There are different types of cats, and different activity levels. Some cats put up with a lot more than others that are very sensitive. Some cat personalities are very forgiving and resilient, but all cats benefit from environmental enrichment.

Identifying your cat's personality helps you know the best ways to help him or her with environmental enrichment. A study from South Australia and New Zealand identified these five broad personality types among cats in The Feline Five: Neuroticism, Extraversion, Impulsive, Agreeableness, and Dominance.

Each of the five types offer a scale of high-to-low extremes. For example, cats that rank very high on neuroticism are the shy sensitive cats that hide more, while those that rank very low on neuroticism are characterized as more bold cats.

How does this impact enrichment? The shy sensitive cats benefit from more hiding spots and quiet spaces so they can get away from the other pets that pester them. Perhaps provide a private room the shy cat can access and chill by himself.

If you have an indoor/outdoor bold adventurous cat, take steps to make sure he's very safe, since he'll be more prone to accidents. When you understand your cat's personality better, you can adjust and enrich the environment appropriately.

EXTRAVERSION

SMART/CURIOUS: Fight boredom with sensory/emotional stimulation

AIMLESS/CLUMSY: Health/age challenges

Extraversion kitties are the very smart, curious cats on one end of the spectrum, while the clumsy, aimless felines fall at the other end of the scale. My Karma-Kat gets bored very easily, so I provide lots of emotional and sensory stimulation for him. It helps that he loves his canine friend, Bravo-Dawg, and they keep each other entertained.

Ranking low on the extraversion scale may indicate a health concern. That's something to check with your veterinarian, especially if the behavior changes suddenly. Very old cats also may become a little bit clumsy or aimless in their activity level.

IMPULSIVE

ERRACTIC/RESTLESS: Professional help

EVEN KEEL: Like routine, well adjusted

Does your impulsive cat behave erratically or act very restless? He may benefit most from consulting with a veterinary behaviorist or a professional animal behavior consultant. Very young cats and kittens naturally act more impulsively, but adult cats should be more settled.

The other extreme on this scale are the cats who love the status quo. Once you've set up a routine for these kitties, they often become easy keepers that stay happy and get along well in the household.

The last two categories are agreeableness and dominance. We sometimes hear more about dominance with dogs, but cats also want to control the situation. One example are the cats that bite to stop petting with the "leave-me-alone" bite.

With any of these extremes, behaviors that disrupt your household can greatly benefit from a behavior professional's advice. It helps you know how to best manage your home environment for your cats.

AGREEABLENESS

FRIENDLY: Well adjusted

IRRITABLE/AGGRESSIVE: Poor socialization, illness/pain/frustration

Cats that rank high on the agreeableness scale are well-adjusted and friendly. Those that rank low can act irritably and aggressively. Irritable or aggressive behavior may be impacted by a variety of issues; poor socialization, perhaps ill health, in pain, or even if cats feel frustrated in some way.

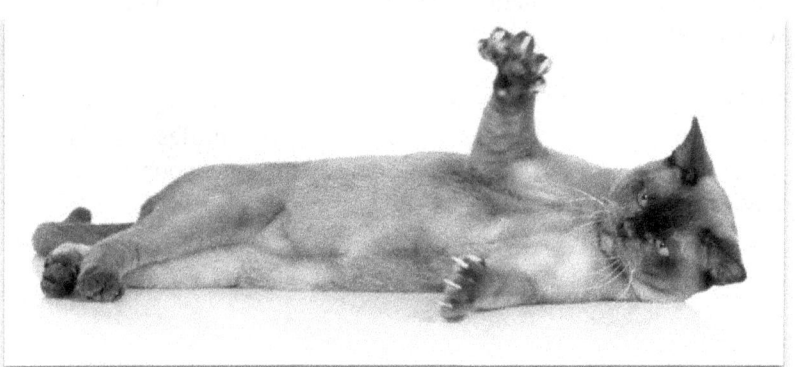

DOMINANCE

BULLY/MOODY: stress, aggression, injury (forced grouping of cats)

A bully or moody personality affects not only the individual cat's behavior, but also the attitude of the other household cats. Injury may cause issues that might be mischaracterized as a dominance behavior.

In forced groupings of cats, some cats may dislike each other or simply need more space to feel comfortable. When forced to share litter boxes, food pans, and sleeping space, stress increases across the board. Environmental enrichment provides a powerful way to relieve stress and fear.

ENVIRONMENTAL ENRICHMENT

Let's get into the nuts and bolts of enriching your cat's environment. Consider home territory first, as this is where most house cats spend the bulk of their lives. Remember to think in terms of your cat as both a predator, and as prey.

Cats need SAFETY for
- Eating
- Drinking
- Sleeping
- Eliminating

Cats need to feel in control in all routine lifestyle activities. Eliminate fear by augmenting the cat's perception of control during eating, drinking, sleeping or eliminating.

For example, imagine Kitty fears his food will be stolen by another cat or the dog. He either eats less and suffers a lack of nutrition, or resorts to scarf-and-barf, where he eats hastily and then stress-vomits somewhere else. Cats concerned about being interrupted during elimination may delay visiting the litter box. That may predispose to urinary tract issues, or prompt inappropriate litter box behaviors.

When planning environmental enrichment, first evaluate your cat's personality. Shy cats benefit from different things than the confident Christopher Columbus type felines.

Map important cat zones. Answer these questions to prioritize your cat's top spots:

1. Where are the litter boxes?
2. What napping and/or lookout spots does he prefer?
3. Where, when, and what does your cat eat?
4. Does she prefer a bowl, fountain, or faucet sip?
5. What legal (and "illegal") scratch ops are available?

VERTICAL SPACE

Second-Story Territory
- Shelves
- Countertops
- Cat Trees
- Stairs
- Windowsills
- Tables & Furniture

Cats are second-story artists who love heights. Why do they like to be up high? Well, it's a way they can see the world, and it's also a safety issue for cats. Oftentimes, the cat that claims the highest perch boasts the highest rank in a particular room or area. So, think about going vertical with environmental enrichment.

SHELVES: Even very small apartments can increase cat territory by extending the space upwards. Clear books off one shelf in your library, for instance, to give the cat a place to lounge and sleep.

COUNTERTOPS: Cats love countertops, but we may not want them near food preparation surfaces. Simply make the illegal area unattractive. Put away food, and cover surfaces with something the cat dislikes, like aluminum foil. Even better, make the LEGAL option more alluring with soft blankets or catnip. If you forbid access to kitchen counters, choose your battles and perhaps provide the cat with his own laundry basket on top of the clothes dryer where it's nice and warm. Environmental enrichment doesn't have to be purchased for a lot of money. Often you can simply adjust placement of existing furniture and cat objects.

CAT TREES: Cat trees are wonderful opportunities that not only provide climbing ops and elevated perches, they offer places for cats to claw and play. Can't afford of fancy-dancy cat tree? Get a cheap ladder. Wrap some sisal rope around the bottom feet, hang cat toys from the steps, place a cat bed or folded towel on the paint rack, and you've got a homemade a cat tree that cats love. If countertops are forbidden, I guarantee a ladder or something that's higher than your countertop will be more cat attractive.

Many cats get along with each other, and sometimes willingly share. However, the greater the number of cats that share space, the more resources you should provide. That reduces the chance they'll argue over who gets to use the "best" cat tree (even if they're identical).

Otherwise, one cat may decide he "owns" every cat tree in the room, even though he can only climb one at a time. Cats can bully and control each other with a simple stare from across the room that prevents the shy feline from accessing the cat tree, or other owned resource. As with litter boxes, placing cat trees in different areas works best.

STAIRS: Do you have a staircase? My cats always love to lounge at the top of the stairs. That provides a high lookout where the cat can watch all the comings and goings of the household. We have a cat tree on the balcony, and also installed a pet gate at the stair landing, to control the dog's movement. The cat-size opening allows easy access to smaller pets, while keeping bigger ones at bay. When you have multiple pets in the home, gates and barriers help manage access to different parts of the house and prevent disputes over resources.

WINDOWS: Many cats yearn for the great outdoors. In too many instances, the dangers and risks outweigh the benefits of offering outside excursions. In our North Texas region, coyotes pose too great a risk. Certainly, you can create "catios" and outdoor entertainment centers for your cat.

Windowsills are wonderful places for cats to lounge and engage with the world outside. Watching birds at feeders or birdbaths, or squirrels and chipmunks provides visual "play" entertainment that helps keep brains youthful. In our case, we rely on "squirrel TV" window watching ops for Karma-Kat.

Here's a caution to consider for some kitties. Remember that cats have both a home range (the inside of your house), plus territory seen through windows they may want to protect. Some cats want to shoo away strange cats seen through the glass and do so with aggressive displays or urine marking. Recognize your cat's personality and whether window watching benefits or frustrates your pet.

HORIZONTAL SPACE

- Litter Box
- Sunny Spots
- Tunnels & Boxes
- Under Beds & Furniture

Yes, cats love to be up high, but think about the horizontal spaces in your home as well. With few exceptions, litter boxes live on the ground level, and are one of your cat's most important territories.

LITTER BOX LOCATION

Location of the litter box can cause or solve many behavior problems. The type, number, and location of the boxes can reduce or increase the angst level in fearful cats. Start with the basics—how many boxes you provide.

I love the 1+1 rule. If you have one cat, then provide one litter box plus one more. If you have two cats, provide two litter boxes plus one. Why does this matter? Many cats prefer to use one box for solid elimination, and the other for liquids. And in multi-cat households, making cats share a single box offers a "bully" cat the ability to guard the facilities and prevent the shy cat from using the bathroom.

When you have only one cat, you may get by with placing the boxes in the same room on opposite sides of the space. Older, ill, or very young cats benefit from litter boxes placed on each level or end of the house, so they can reach the facilities more quickly.

It's better, however, to offer litter boxes in different rooms, especially when you have more than one kitty. Otherwise, one cat (or the nosy dog!) could block a doorway where all the litter boxes live. By placing litter boxes in spaces some distance apart, you've enriched the environment by offering cats control of when and where they can safely eliminate.

Think about the cat as prey when choosing the type of box and where to place them. When stuck in corers of rooms, deep inside closets, or under furniture, the location can be easily guarded by one cat. Or, the shy cat might fear being ambushed and trapped by a bully pet during elimination.

Covered boxes may also be off-putting to shy or fearful cats. They can feel like traps, hold offensive odors, or prevent the "posing" cat to see danger approaching. The midway point of a room or wall offers one of the best locations for an environmentally friendly litter box. In this location, cats can see when it's occupied, danger approaching, and easily escape.

SUN WORSHIPERS

Think about sunny spots. My Karma-Kat loves to sleep on the glass tabletop in the morning sun. How many cats follow that puddle of sunshine across the carpet each morning and afternoon?

Homes without large windows can duplicate sunny delight with light fixtures and heating pads. After my old lady cat, Seren, celebrated her 19th birthday, we moved her bed permanently to the dining room table beneath the stain glass lamp. Older cats like Seren particularly enjoy warmth that helps creaky arthritic joints move more readily.

Why not provide a heating pad beneath a thick layer of blankets or towels for soothing your golden oldie kitty's aches? That may help the cat's ability to self-groom and climb in and out of the litter box. Cats of any age love warmth.

TUNNELS & BOXES

Cats like hiding spots to lurk, play, ambush your ankles, or stay away from danger. If you have a shy kitty who spends time under the bed, boxes and tunnels are some of the best enrichment tools you can offer. Having lots of options for hiding, or scurrying from place to place through hidden tunnels, gives the cat control. He doesn't have to risk being seen in order to get from point A (litter box), to point B (food dish), for example.

Remember, it's all about the *perception* of danger and control. If your cat loves hiding under the bed, let her do that. In addition, provide a tunnel or series of taped-together boxes for her to run from the bed into the next room. Give her lots of options to hide and snuggle. One box won't cut it. Offer several in each room.

FURNITURE LURKERS

Don't like the look of boxes? How about covering tables with floor-length tablecloths instead? If your cat won't use a cat tree, perhaps place a box or bed under a table or on top of the piano to explore. My cat Karma lurks under end tables to tease and ambush the dog, what fun! He also uses the backs of chairs and tabletops to cross the room, to stay out of dog-sniffing range. Listen to your cat by watching what he or she chooses.

With practice, cats build confidence as each success teaches them the benefits of being brave. That in turn reduces the stress levels in the cat.

HITTING THE MARK

- Scratching
- Climbing
- Cheek-rubbing
- Middening

Cats mark their owned territory with both visual and scent reminders. Now, if we're fortunate, they forgo urine spraying. To spray, cats back up to a (usually) vertical object, the tail shivers, and urine sprays backwards to coat the object with signature scent. Both the boy cats and girl kitties urine-mark, although it's most typical of intact males.

Cats may still posture and go through the tail-shaking, back-up-to-the-furniture display, thankfully without the liquid spray. More rarely, cats leave feces uncovered as a territorial mark of ownership.

Obviously, using urine or feces to shout about their ownership does not appeal to humans. But cats mark with other techniques, too, and you cannot—and you should not—attempt to stop them. Give the cats legal opportunities to do what comes naturally. That gives them control over the environment, which naturally lessens stress.

Cats scratch to mark objects with their claws. Even those without claws go through the motions. The claws and paws leave both visual and scented Post-It notes telling other cats of their presence.

Finally, cats use allo-marking (face and body rubbing) to deposit scent on important territory. Cats have scent glands in their cheeks, chins, and foreheads, as well as the tail area.

That's why Kitty takes great pains to rub against doorways, or even favored humans and other cats with whole-body rubs and tail wraps. These scented marks spread pheromones that communicate to other cats, identifying the object (or the other creature) as familiar, and therefore safe.

What and where do cats tend to mark? Important objects and locations include the cat's scratch post, areas on or adjacent to vital cat pathways and lookouts (such as windows or stairs), and places the cat sleeps, eats, or toilets.

Scratching targets and favorite cheek-rub areas tell you what your cat considers to be most important. Listen to your cats, and they'll point you to exactly where they need a scratch object, in order to mark and claim the territory. If you don't want Kitty scratching the chair next to the window, try replacing the chair with something better, like a scratching perching object. Your cat wants to claim that window lookout as his personal space, after all.

Also think about the types of surfaces that appeal the most to your cat's claws and duplicate those textures on the legal object. If she targets upholstery, choose a legal target that matches that surface.

To feel in control of the environment, Kitty leaves marks proclaiming, "Kilroy-Kitty was here!" Even when you don't see outside stray cats or other critters, your cat's *perception* of threat matters most. Giving him options to become a confident, cat in control helps reduce stress, which in turn means he'll have less need to mark and shout his ownership to the world. Your furniture will thank you.

COMPANIONSHIP

- Cats Don't Do Force
- Kitty Control
- Frequent & Short = Best
- LISTEN to the Cat!

Believe it or not, cats consider YOU a vital and important part of owned territory. Why else would he cheek-rub you, groom your hair, or even (yikes!) turn your leg into a scratching post? For that reason, companionship should be included in your enrichment plan. As with other considerations, listen to your cat to figure out what he wants. Misunderstandings (on both sides!) can raise everyone's stress and potentially damage your relationship.

AFFECTION ON KITTY'S TERMS

So you want your cat to sit on your lap? I hear clients complain that Kitty doesn't want to snuggle, or, "I want to rub his tummy."

Forcing cats into hugs, or on your lap takes away the cat's control. That results in increased stress, possibly fear, potential bites, and could teach your cat to avoid you.

Cats are not dogs, and rarely enjoy tummy rubs. Trust me on this. Even if they show you their tummy, tempting you to touch that sweet, soft spot, please refrain. While rolling on the ground and baring the tummy can be a kitty invitation for attention, touching the cat's belly often prompts a bite or bunny-claw-kick response. After all, the posture puts all four clawed paws and teeth in an action-ready defensive pose.

KNOW KITTY'S PREFERENCES

Cats love you but still want to control the interaction. By allowing them this freedom, you'll encourage cats to interact more frequently.

Here's an example. My Karma-Kat does NOT like to be picked up and held. But he will decide to lap sit on his own, usually while I work at my computer (but never in front of the TV in the evenings). He also prefers to interact with me while I'm in bed. That way, I'm confined by the covers and he can control how close to get and the duration of the contact. This is our "face time" literally, when he cheek-rubs my face, and ultimately settles in the curve behind my knees for us to sleep together.

What prime times do your cats seeks your attention? Cloudy and colder days seem to increase the inclination for lap-sitting, even when cats avoid it at other times. Also, if you routinely ignore or spurn your cat's solicitation for attention, Kitty begins to do the same to you. By giving the cat a head-scratch or interactive game of chase-the-feather when she asks, the cat also becomes more likely to agree to your requests for petting.

Think about frequent but short sessions. Pay attention to how cats solicit and give attention to each other. During mutual grooming, cats target each other's head and back of the neck—hard-to-reach places a cat can't groom by himself. When petting your cat, focus on these favorite spots with only brief contact of two or three strokes, and wait for Kitty to ask for more.

A full body stroke sometimes is too much of a good thing for a cat. These cats beg and beg for pets, but then after only a stroke or two, they bite your hand to stop the interaction. While they love your attention, the actual contact and repeated strokes can overstimulate. It's best to leave the cat wanting more, and you can offer additional attention with long-distance toys.

Listen by watching kitty body signals. Ears turn sideways like airplane wings, or the tail becomes active when the cat's done with petting. You'll quickly learn to understand your individual cat's signals just by paying attention, so you can stop contact before Kitty drives home his preferences with tooth and claw.

Cats don't need to snuggle to express their affection. Sitting across the room and gazing at you with adoration may be the ultimate way to say, "I love you." If that's your cat, then enjoy the time spent together with Kitty lounging on the back of your chair, rather than in your arms.

CAT-TO-CAT (AND OTHER) COMPANIONS

- "I own this!" squabbles
- Timeshare
- Familiarity vs. Stranger-Danger
- Safety Issues

Many folks can't get by with a single kitty. However, the single most stressful impact on a cat's life is OTHER CATS! That doesn't mean you must limit your furry love. But it does mean that the more cats you have, the more resources and environmental enrichment you'll need.

If you have a very gregarious even-keel cat, that actually may help your shy cat come out of her shell. There's a reason for the term "copy-cat" and both kittens and adult cats duplicate behaviors patterned after other animal friends.

At my house, Karma-Kat expects a treat if the dog gets one and has learned several of the dog obedience commands just by watching his canine buddy perform.

Other cats, especially even-tempered felines, can serve as enrichment to your other cats. Adopting pairs of bonded cats or kittens offers a stress buffer because they already know each other. Young kittens adopted together keep each other entertained so they don't target grumpy or shy cats with their playful antics. You need to judge this based on the personality of the cats you have, particularly during introductions.

TIMESHARE MENTALITY

In multi-cat households, disputes over resources often arise. Every cat likes to think he or she owns and controls everything. For example, one cat may control the top of the television set, while another cat owns the bedroom, and yet a third cat sits at the top of the stairs and controls everything from a distance with wide-eyed stares.

With fewer resources, cats that get along well must learn to share resources, while still feeling in control. It works this way: If cat #1 "owns" the cat tree but isn't present to use it, cat #2 feels safe enough to lounge. Then when cat#1 returns, the cat "borrowing" the cat tree quickly relinquishes claim, so no argument takes place.

Not all cats agree to timeshare. Therefore, the greater the number of cats you have, the more resources you should provide. That reduces the chance they'll argue over who gets to use the "best" bed (even if all the beds are identical).

Remember the 1+1 rule for numbers of litter boxes, scratch posts, beds, and the like. Increase the resources so there's less for the cats to squabble over.

What if your tiny apartment can't accommodate half a dozen litter boxes, or cat trees? Again, listen to the cats. Those felines that already sleep together and groom each other may be willing to share some resources. Perhaps you have five cats, but three of them sleep together, and the other pair groom each other. In this case, you may get by with treating each friendly group of cats as one entity that shares a single jumbo-size litter box, for example. Familiar friendly cats share and show willingness by spending time together.

SAFETY ALWAYS!

The odd-cat-out doesn't spend time with the others and gets picked on. Cats that sleep together or groom each other smell alike. Felines that smell different don't share that "safe" group signature scent and may be shunned. Sadly, that's not unusual, but it does raise the stress level in the pariah cat.

Again, offering lots of hiding spots, cat tunnels, and sometimes pheromone products that ease tension can help. Offering the bully cats more to do, with toys and food puzzles, helps take the target off the picked-on cat.

You'll find more advice on introductions to other cats, dogs, babies and humans in <u>My Cat Hates My Date! Teach Cats to Accept Babies, Toddlers & Lovers</u> <u>(A Quick-Tips Guide Book 2).</u>

FEEDING ENRICHMENT

In October of 2018, the [American Association of Feline Practitioners](#) (CatVets.com) released a practice guidelines statement, a consensus statement on [how to feed cats](#). Now, you would think that would be easy when you just open the can or bag and drop food into the bowl. Who knew, we could be so wrong!

For years and years, we've fed cats the same way. We set up a feeding station probably in the kitchen or laundry room. If we have two or three cats, we offer enough food in a big bowl for all of them. Or if generous, we offer several little bowls side by side. If the never-ending bowl isn't available 24/7, then we might feed them in the morning, and again in the evening after work.

When we listen to our cats, though, that's not a species appropriate way to feed them. Cats are naturally solitary hunters and eaters. They eat one mouse-size meal at a time. In a natural setting, a cat may spend a good portion of his day hunting to try to find that one mouse.

Today we have great nutritional information for cats published by a host of veterinary nutritionists, researchers, and pet food companies. But until this consensus statement came out, we mostly relied on word of mouth or trial and error how best to feed cats.

As it happens, feeding cats naturally falls into environmental enrichment. It improves the health of your cat both physically and emotionally to feed in a species appropriate way.

We all know that meat is number one on the cat's want- and need-to-eat list. In terms of environmental enrichment, the kind of food is vital, but equally important is *how* you feed.

Because cats are solitary munchers, to obtain the calories they need, they must eat small meals multiple times a day. That means if you feed multiple cats at the same time in the same space, you can drastically increase stress levels. The cat has lost control of when, where, and how much to eat when he must sit next to another feline and compete for food.

A BETTER WAY TO FEED

The consensus statement urges us to 1) feed cats separately, 2) provide multiple water stations, and 3) feed small meals several times a day.

Just as with other resources, spread out the feeding stations and water fountains. Otherwise, one cat could guard and prevent access if all the food bowls and fountains are in a single room. At my house, we provide water bowls at every sink in the house. We also have two cat water fountains on tabletops, and another on the floor for the dog that (of course!) the cat often prefers.

With a single cat, you can divide the daily ration into five or more mouse-size meals. Dry food can be served on paper plates or saucers in different spots around the house. Try placing a meal on the top of a cat tree, to entice Kitty to climb up for exercise, with that food reward as a bonus.

When cats must "work" for their kibble, they exercise their body and mind, keeping interest engaged which in turn lowers stress. Hiding the meals in different spots turns meals into a fun challenge, so cats use their natural hunting abilities.

But how do you handle feeding several cats multiple meals in different areas of the house? Or in our case, how do you keep the dog from finding and scarfing up all the kitty vittles?

All kinds of cat foraging tools and food puzzles are now available. These mimic the way cats obtain food on the wild side and can be helpful to slim down tubby tabbies.

I feed my Karma-Kat with mouse-shaped puzzle toys that I hide around the house. They can be hidden inside boxes, on shelves, in cat tunnels, at the top of chair backs, or balanced on doorknobs. He must find the toy, and then shake out the kibble to eat. Wet food, which is more species-appropriate, can be smeared into textured feeding mats, smushed into forage feeders, or placed inside refrigerated feeders that keep perishable food fresh and open on a timer.

Our 120-pound dog can easily reach cat puzzle toys set high on countertops. To keep the dog from raiding the cat food, I use door barriers that allow Karma-Kat access, but keep the dog at bay. For cat households with smaller dogs, use the cat's second-story territory to set out water stations and puzzle toys beyond canine sniffing range.

Monitor all your cats' eating habits. You'll need to provide puzzle toys or stations in multiples of five or more per cat, per day. Identify which cat holds sway in each part of the house and situate at least five feeders in each of these areas.

For example, the cat that owns the dining room would have access to the five puzzle toys in that area, while the cat that loves the upstairs office would be provided with her own five rations in and around her favorite lounging areas. By providing puzzle toys and foraging options in a variety of locations, cats may be able to graze and hunt as needed, but without one cat hoarding all the bounty.

For very young, very old, or ill cats with special nutritional needs, don't hesitate to sequester these kitties to ensure they get appropriation nutrition. Once they've eaten, they can again co-mingle with the rest of the clowder.

You know your cats best. So, use what works best in your situation, and adjust as needed.

HEALTHY EXTRAS FOR FUN

Sight
- Window Watching
- Bird Baths & Feeders
- Stalking the Red Dot
- Wands & Lure Toys

Sound
- Fountains, Chimes, Birds
- TV & Recordings
- "Crackle" & Bell Toys

Scent
- Catnip
- Valerian
- Silver Vine
- Pheromone Products

Taste
- "Leaf" Me Alone!
- Flower Power

Touch
- Ladders
- Ropes
- Self-groomers

Cats play for exercise, to practice normal cat behaviors, and because it's just plain fun. One of the best ways to relieve feline stress is through play therapy. Interactive play with your cat also enhances the bond of love and affection you share.

Part of play and stalking behavior includes silent watching. For older cats and some shy felines, simply watching the feather lure toy move, while other cats interact, also offers benefits. So, don't think your cat doesn't like play. If Kitty watches you or others interact, you've achieved a positive effect.

Set up an easily cleaned area in the kitchen, bathroom, or the laundry. Fill a box with leaves for the cat to play with, or scatter leaves across the floor. Double up with food treats underneath the leaves to increase the fun. As the cat explores and enjoys the smells, sounds, and sights as he paw-swipes the leaves, he suddenly finds treats—bonus for the cat! You can create your own foraging and puzzle fun without buying pricy options from a pet supply store.

Are you handy? Create a cat tree using real branches. We have about 13 acres and cut cedar logs to bring inside for cat scratching ops. The cedar bark shreds and makes a mess that cats absolutely love. Remember: scratching visually marks territory, too, so making a mess offers another level of feline joy.

Toys and games are anything that cats find entertaining, and often cost nothing. Engage all the cat's senses: sight, sound, touch, taste, and scent. Find toys and games that address more than one of these sensory delights.

We have lots of windows at our house. Wildlife shares our 13 acres, and a colony of squirrels uses the patio roof as a racetrack directly outside my office window. Karma-Kat sits on the desk and chatters back at the squirrels and birds that go by. I call it "cat TV."

Both Karma and the dog run to check the window if I call, "bunny-bunny-bunny" (my name for window-viewing pleasures). What word(s) do you use to alert your cats to fun stuff? Karma-Kat comes running from anywhere in the house when he hears this announcement.

For example, when a noisy hailstorm blew in, I announced "bunny-bunny-bunny." Instead of fearing the loud battering sound and weird sight, Karma-Kat paw-chased the bouncing ice from his side of the windowpane, as though they were Ping-Pong balls sent for his entertainment.

What if you don't have access to acreage or wildlife? How about positioning bird baths and feeders near your windows? Hummingbirds come to high rise apartment windows if the feeder is available.

High-definition televisions allow cats to see and recognize wildlife as though it's a window. Tune your TV or tablet to videos to see if your cats react. Don't forget to turn up the sound. Cats hear things outside of human's sound sense, so you'll be amazed what the cat may react to. However, some cats may become frustrated by inability to catch the image, so do supervise and adjust based on your pet's individual behavior.

What about battery-powered and electronic toys? They can help keep your cats entertained when you must be away. Some interface with your phone, so you can "talk" to your pet from work.

Ideally, though, play interactive games in person with your cat so they identify the fun stuff with your presence. That's not only stress relief for them, but also calming and fun for you. My Karma-Kat isn't interested in stalking the red dot, probably because the dog has become obsessed with catching it. So, he instead enjoys watching the dog's antics.

Karma-Kat's favorites are fishing-pole lure toys and feather wands. He also enjoys "carpet-surfing" when we drag a towel or blanket across the floor, and he jumps on for a ride. Another favorite is a self-grooming brush made especially for cats. The brush, formed in an inverted U-shape, sits on a solid platform for cats to cheek-rub and body-stroke as they wish. It feels good to him, plus leaves signature scent marks.

Water fountains offer more than drinking ops. Some kitties love to dabble paws in the water. The sound of gurgling provides a soothing sound for cats and humans alike. We've added windchimes outside on the patio that offer movement for cat enjoyment and pretty sounds. For cats that enjoy stuffy-type toys for munching and pouncing, try offering crinkle-toys that make noises when bitten. The more sensory delights you can offer, the better.

If you don't have safe outdoor places for cats to play, bring the green inside. Grow cat grass, offer fresh or dried catnip, valerian, silver vine, or mint for the cat's smelling pleasure. Today we know that the kitty smell sense rivals that of many dogs, and cats enjoy recreational sniffing. (See CatsAndSquirrels.com for a fun study) If you've got toys your cat ignores, drop them inside a sealed baggy full of fresh catnip and allow to marinate overnight. For felines that love the 'nip, that's a sure-fire way to refresh toy interest.

Offer cat pheromones to reduce cat stress. Several products are available. Some help specifically with territorial issues that identify areas as cat-owned and "safe." Others address intercat aggression. I recommend the Feliway and ComfortZone products but there are a number of others now available that use scent and pheromones to great effect.

While some flowers and plants pose dangers to cats (beware lilies!), edible plants provide enjoyment for both cats and their humans. Think about bringing in a basket of blooms or bouquet of cat-safe flowers, like roses, for your cats to enjoy. They can pluck the petals and make a mess you can easily vacuum up later.

FEAR FREE TRAINING

KNOW THE TRIGGERS
- Stress Free Vet Visits
- Stranger Danger!
- Crate Expectations
- Clicker Training

After covering territory, companionship, food, and care, let's dive further into feline fear, and how to help your cat feel safe. Most cats feel anxiety and stress when taken outside of their home range (their house). Travel from home happens most commonly for veterinary clinic visits.

To address this, you'll find specific help advice in <u>My Cat Hates My Vet! Foiling Fear Before, During & After Vet Visits</u> (<u>A Quick-Tips Guide Book 3</u>).

That said, your cat's home range also can prompt anxious behavior, stress, or downright fear. Environmental enrichment techniques included in this book help a great deal to diffuse fear-driven triggers. Look further, though, to identify and plan for more specific causes of kitty angst.

VISITING MONSTERS

Does your Christopher Columbus Cat love exploring and meeting holiday guests who visit your home? Or do you know Shrinking Violet Cat won't appreciate stranger-danger invading her turf?

Give your cats a break and set limits for your human visitors before they arrive. Aunt Ethel does not need to snuggle your cat. And while cat-savvy kids may be respectful of your cat's feelings, the toddler grandkids often can't resist chasing (and terrorizing) your feline friends.

Frankly, it's easier to train cats than many humans. Take the choice away from your guests, especially if they can't follow direction. Give your cats their own private space, with a room that's off limits to humans.

CRATE EXPECTATIONS

Know the triggers. One of the biggest is the appearance of the cat carrier or crate. It takes only one experience for your cat to know that when the carrier appears, he'll be shoved inside, taken away from safety, and handled by strangers who stick thermometers into rude places.

With environmental enrichment, turn that carrier from a fear-filled trigger into a safe joyful destination. That helps you reduce fear when traveling with Kitty beyond his home turf. Here's how.

Don't hide the carrier away. Make it part of the furniture and leave the door open or off. When the carrier stays in sight all the time, it loses power to scare cats. Put favorite toys or treats inside for the cat to discover during foraging adventures. That becomes an instant reward for exploring and acting confident. Use pheromone products to help cats accept the carriers as safe havens in their territory.

At my house, we perch three cat carriers on top of an enormous dog crate. Karma-Kat's food puzzle toys are rotated and hidden in each of the carriers, so he goes in and out of them frequently. Adding a snuggly blanket inside, or draping a towel over the opening, invites cats to use the carrier as a bed or hidey-hole.

By doing this, cats no longer identify carriers with vet visits, and that reduces fear and stress. Car rides may also be scary, but the fear factor goes down when the cat carrier feels safe for your cat.

Choosing a [Cat Friendly Practice](https://catvets.com/cfp/cfp) and/or one that ascribes to [Fear Free](https://fearfreepets.com/) techniques ensures the veterinarian and staff go the extra mile to reduce fear, anxiety, and stress in your cat.

CLICKER TRAINING

Training also builds confidence and reduces fear. Clicker training works for cats just like it does for dogs, or horses, or dolphins, or any other critter. The clicker marks a behavior that you like, and you partner that CLICK-sound with a reward. Dogs often learn most quickly with a treat-reward they only get during training. With cats, the reward may be a treat, or a feather toy, or anything else the cat relishes.

Clicker training works great for cats, because they won't be coerced. Rather than try to force the cat, simply watch for a behavior you like. For example, he sits, you CLICK! and give a reward and the cat says, "Oh, hey, I kind of like this click stuff because I'm in control. If I sit, that makes her give me a treat." That gives your cat control of the situation, to build kitty confidence, reduce stress, and prevent fear.

Keep training sessions very short. Ask your cat to repeat the exercise only a few times. Always end on a positive note so Kitty looks forward to another play-training game.

THANK YOU FOR READING!

Dear Reader,

I began writing about pets more than twenty years ago—in dog years I should be dead! I hope you enjoyed reading **DOES MY CAT HATE ME?** and that it's helped you answer that question correctly—your cat LOVES you! And now you know how to show kitty you love him or her back.

For cat-to-cat angst and a whole lot more feline behavior tips and tricks, find detailed how-to answers in the full length book, **COMPETABILITY: SOLVING BEHAVIOR PROBLEMS IN YOUR MULTI-CAT HOUSEHOLD.**

Many times, I hear from readers who share stories about their dogs and cats, and I'd love to hear from you. Maybe YOUR pet's heartwarming story could be published on my blog or even included in a future book. All cats deserve to be famous!

I'd like to ask a big favor—could you please post a review of this book (loved it, hated it) as I'd enjoy your feedback. You may not realize how much influence readers like you have to make or break a book simply by sharing your thoughts in a review. So if you have the time, here's a link to my author page on Amazon where you can find all my books: http://tinyurl.com/m92z83c

Thank you so much for spending your time with me. Now…go pet your pets!

Amy Shojai is an IAABC certified animal behavior consultant and a nationally known authority on pet care. She is the award-winning author of more than 30 cat and dog books and thousands of articles and columns.

In the past she created the Puppies.About.com site and was the behavior expert at Cats.About.com. Amy regularly appears on national radio and TV including Animal Planet DOGS 101 and CATS 101.

Amy addresses a wide range of fun-to-serious issues in her work, covering training, behavior, health care, and medical topics. She also writes the September Day "Thrillers With Bite" dog viewpoint series featuring a trained Maine Coon cat and German Shepherd service dog.

She and her husband live with Karma-Kat, Bravo-Dawg, and the enduring memory of Magic the German Shepherd and Siamese "wannabe" Seren-Kitty.

Amy can be reached at her website at www.shojai.com where you can subscribe to her PET PEEVES Newsletter and Ask Amy YouTube Channel, like her on Facebook.com/amyshojai.cabc, follow on Twitter @amyshojai, and check out her Bling, Bitches & Blood Blog at AmyShojai.com.

www.ingramcontent.com/pod-product-compliance
Lightning Source LLC
Chambersburg PA
CBHW071727020426
42333CB00017B/2423